A Beginners Guide to Algorithm Analysis

By: Randerson112358

Also, by Randerson112358

YouTube :
https://www.youtube.com/channel/UCaV_0qp2NZd319K
4_K8Z5SQ

YouTube (Programming):
https://www.youtube.com/channel/UCbmb5IoBtHZTpYZ
CDBOC1CA

Website:
http://everythingcomputerscience.com/

Contents

Chapter 0: What this book is about

0.1 Background

I have spent many years programming and in the Information Technology field. My main field of study was Computer science also known as (CS). Computer science is the study of the principles and use of computers. Simply put it's the science that deals with the theory and methods of processing information in digital computers, the design of computer hardware and software, and the applications of computers. A computer is simply a tool for a computer scientist, like a telescope for an astronomer. Humans can do everything a computer can do, but computers can usually do the computations much faster and with more accuracy.

Computer science has many interesting specializations that include Artificial Intelligence (AI), which is the theory and development of computers to perform tasks that normally require human intelligence such as visual perception, speech recognition, decision making and translation between languages. This amazing field also has specializations in Computer Programming (make desktop apps and games), Computer Engineering (design computer hardware), Mobile Development (make apps), Game Design (think Xbox, Nintendo, etc.), Graphics (think Toy Story, Frozen, Harry Potter, Star Wars), Data Analytics/Science (see patterns and make predictions of the future from data) and Databases (store lots of information).

In computer science you must write many algorithms for the computer to perform different tasks. When writing these algorithms, it can be hard to compare two programs or algorithms that perform the same task but using different steps. For example, I could have an algorithm that tells a robot to fetch me an apple and my friend Nick could have a similar algorithm for a robot, however my robot may first exit the house then walk over to a store and buy the apple for me, while Nick's robot simply goes to the refrigerator and grabs an apple for me. Nick's robot took less steps to get the same result. So which algorithm is better? We can use algorithm analysis to get an unbiased opinion of how efficient an algorithm is.

Students complain often that algorithm analysis is difficult and abstract. Often some of them ask about the importance of algorithm analysis to computer science, computational tool development and software engineering, so what is the significance of algorithm analysis to the development of computational software? Analysis of algorithms more specifically the computational complexity is very important, because programmers care about the efficiency of an algorithm in terms of time, space, and sometimes energy. A computer program is no good to us if it takes one thousand years to perform a task as it is likely that the person that started the task will no longer be around.

This brings us to what this book is about. In this book I intend to teach you some of the methods and tricks you can use to solve and analyze these algorithms. This book will provide you with easy to use techniques and an understanding to solve many different algorithms and their runtime complexities in terms such as Big-Oh (**O**), Big Theta (**Θ**), and Big Omega (**Ω**). You will need basic understanding of imperative programming as I will be switching between different languages and even pseudo code, algebra, and summations. I plan on helping you learn this material fast and efficiently just like the algorithms we want to use in our daily lives. Let's get started!

Chapter 1: What is an algorithm

1.1 Introduction

An algorithm is any well-defined procedure that takes some value or set of values as input and produces some value or set of values as output. – Thomas H. Cormen, Chales E. Leiserson (2009). The word algorithm can be traced back to a mathematician named Abdullah Muhammad bin Musa al-Khwarizmi born in Persia, whom is cited as "the father of algebra". He was the most read about mathematician in Europe during the middle ages and he introduced the number system we use today.

The word algorithm is also a synonym for procedure, program, method, and function. You can think of an algorithm like a recipe used to cook food, it is just a set of instructions. As an example, in the case of making a cake using a recipe A.K.A your algorithm, your input may be eggs, flower, sugar etc. and your output is a cake!

Types of algorithms

Algorithms are being used everywhere, from your recipes used to cook that delicious meal, to giving shoppers the minimum amount of change. Algorithms are used in games and to sort data and objects. The list goes on. One important algorithm is being tested to diagnose breast cancer from the images of mammograms using a technique called machine learning or ML for short, and you may have heard of self-driving cars, yes there is an algorithm that helps the car to perform that task. Below is a list of a few algorithms that you may have heard of before, if not then please allow me to be the first to introduce them to you.

Greedy Algorithm

Have you ever wondered how cashiers know the least amount of change to give back? Sure, some people can do it in their heads, but for others the computer tells them the exact amount of US coins to give back. This algorithm uses a greedy approach and is called a greedy algorithm. Specifically, a greedy algorithm to make change and give the least amount of coins back. Greedy algorithms produce good solutions on some mathematical problems, but not on others. An example of this would be a greedy algorithm trying to make the least amount of change for a coin set like { 1, 2, 4, 5 } where it would fail when trying to make change for 8, instead of giving back two 4 coins, the algorithm would return a 5 coin, a 2 coin and a 1 coin, because it will choose to use the greatest value first (coin 5), but the same greedy algorithm is great for using the US coin set {1, 5, 10, 25, 50}, where it always returns the least amount of coins.

In general, greedy algorithms have five components:

1. A candidate (set, list, etc) from which a solution is created.
2. A selection function, which chooses the best candidate to be added to the solution.
3. A feasibility function, that is used to determine if a candidate can be used to contribute to a solution.
4. An object function, which assigns a value to a solution, or a partial solution.
5. A solution function, which will indicate when we have discovered a complete solution.

Greedy algorithms should be applied to problems exhibiting the greedy choice property and the optimal substructure property.

Greedy choice property: We can make whatever choice seems best now and then solve the subproblems that arise later. The choice made by a greedy algorithm may depend on choices made so far but not on future choices or all the solutions to the subproblem. It iteratively makes one greedy choice after another, reducing each given problem into a smaller one. In other words, a greedy algorithm never reconsiders its choices. This is the main difference from dynamic programming, which is exhaustive and is guaranteed to find the solution. After every stage, dynamic programming makes decisions based on all the decisions made in the previous stage and may reconsider the previous stage's algorithmic path to solution.

Optimal substructure: A problem exhibits optimal substructure if an optimal solution to the problem contains optimal solutions to the sub-problems.

The C-Program for the greedy algorithm is below:

```
1.   #include<stdio.h>
2.   #define LEN  4 // The CONSTANT length of our array/coin set
3.
4.   //Greedy Algorithm for printing the least amount of change
5.   void greedy(int amount);
6.
7.   int main(void){
8.
9.      int amount = 99;
10.     greedy(amount);
11.     system("pause");//Comment this out if you are not using Windows
12.  }
13.
14.  void greedy(int amount){
15.
16.     int i=0;//index of the array
17.     int number;//the number of least amount of coin for a specific coin value
18.     int coin_set[LEN]= {25, 10, 5, 1};//The USD coin set
19.
20.     printf("The least amount of change needed for the amount %d is below: \n", amount);
21.
22.     while(i < LEN){
23.
24.       if(coin_set[i] <= amount){
25.         number = amount/coin_set[i];
26.
27.         //Prints the least number of coins needed
28.         if(coin_set[i] == 25 ){
29.           printf("%d quarters (%d) \n", number, coin_set[i]);
30.         }
31.         if(coin_set[i] == 10 ){
32.           printf("%d dimes (%d) \n", number, coin_set[i]);
33.         }
34.         if(coin_set[i] == 5 ){
35.           printf("%d nickels (%d) \n", number, coin_set[i]);
36.         }
37.         if(coin_set[i] == 1 ){
38.           printf("%d pennies (%d) \n", number, coin_set[i]);
39.         }
40.
41.         amount = amount - number *coin_set[i];
42.       }
43.
44.       i++;//increment i by 1
45.     }
46.  }
```

Divide and Conquer Algorithms

Let's look at a fun divide and conquer algorithm used for the number guessing game. To play the guessing game, a person (player A) will choose a random number from n to m, another person (player B) will have to guess player A's number in "x" turns. Player A will assist player B by telling player B if the number they guessed is higher than or lower than player A's randomly chosen number. The Algorithm will tell you if it is possible to guess player A's number in the given amount of turns x and will tell the maximum amount of tries or guesses you will need to guess there number correctly. The Number Guessing Game uses binary search to quickly find a solution. A binary search is a dichotomic divide and conquer search algorithm. The maximum number of turns it takes to guess a number from 1 to 100 is $\log_2(100 - 1 + 1) = \log_2(100) = 7$. Hence the worst case running time is $\log_2(Max - Min + 1)$.

An example of how the game works:

Player A: I am thinking of a number from 1 to 100, can you guess my number within 7 turns?
Player B: Sure, is your number 89?
Player A: Nope guess a lower number.
Player B: Okay, is your number 75?
Player A: Nope, guess a higher number.
Player B: Okay is your number 80?
Player A: Nope, guess a higher number.

Player B: Okay, is your number 88?
Player A: Yes, congratulations you guessed my number in 4 turns you win!

The C-Program for the number guessing game algorithm is below:

```
1.   # include <stdio.h>
2.   # include <stdlib.h>
3.   # include <math.h>   // Library used for math in this case log() and ciel()
4.
5.   int main(void)
6.   {
7.       //Declaring Variables to be used
8.       int lowRange = 1;
9.       int highRange = 100;
10.      int possibleGuesses = highRange + lowRange - 1;
11.      int maxTurns = (int)(log(possibleGuesses)/log(2)) + 1; // = log base 2 of possible guesses by rules of logarithms
12.      int yourGuess;
13.      int playerAnswer;
14.      int countNumTurns = 1;
15.
16.      printf("Choose a number from %d to %d.\n", lowRange, highRange);
17.      printf("I will guess your number in %d turns or less.\n\n", maxTurns );
18.
19.          //This loops through the algorithm
20.      do{
21.          possibleGuesses = highRange + lowRange - 1;
22.          yourGuess = (int) ceil(possibleGuesses / 2.0);
23.
24.          printf("Is your number %d ?\n",yourGuess );
25.          printf("Press (1) Yes (2) Guess a lower number (3) Guess a higher number\n");
26.                  scanf("%d", &playerAnswer);
27.
28.          if(playerAnswer == 3)//Guess was to low
29.              lowRange = yourGuess + 1;
30.          if(playerAnswer == 2) // Guess was too high
31.              highRange = yourGuess - 1;
32.          if (playerAnswer == 1)
33.              break;
34.
35.              countNumTurns++;
36.
37.          }while(playerAnswer != 1 && countNumTurns <= maxTurns);
38.
39.      //Print the end results
40.      if(countNumTurns > maxTurns)
41.          printf("You made a mistake somewhere, you've exceeded the maximum turns. \n");
42.      else
43.      printf("I guessed your number in %d turns !\n", countNumTurns );
44.
45.
```

```
46.    system("pause"); //This is only for windows operating system otherwise comment it out.
47. }
```

Sorting Algorithms

In computer science a sorting algorithm is an algorithm that puts elements of a list in a certain order. Almost any list that comes out of a computer is sorted into some sort of order, and there are many more sorted lists inside computers that the user doesn't see. Many clever algorithms have been devised for putting values into order efficiently like bubble sort, selection sort, and merge sort.

Those are just a few of the many algorithms out there, but they are no good to us if they aren't efficient and take a very long time to run, luckily, we can analyze them asymptotically!

Chapter 2: Asymptotic notations

2.1 Asymptotic introduction

Asymptotic Notation is a method of describing limiting behavior that allow us to analyze an algorithm's execution time by identifying its behavior as the input size 'n' for the algorithm grows or increases. This is the algorithm's growth rate. Does the algorithm execute relatively quickly as the input size increases? How slow will the algorithm become when the input size grows? With Asymptotic Notation we will be able to answer these questions and be able to compare programs, algorithms and their efficiency. Types of asymptotic notations are **Big-O (O)**, **Big Theta (Θ)**, and **Big Omega (Ω)**, **Little-O**, and **Little Omega** they are all just sets of functions.

Big-O (O)

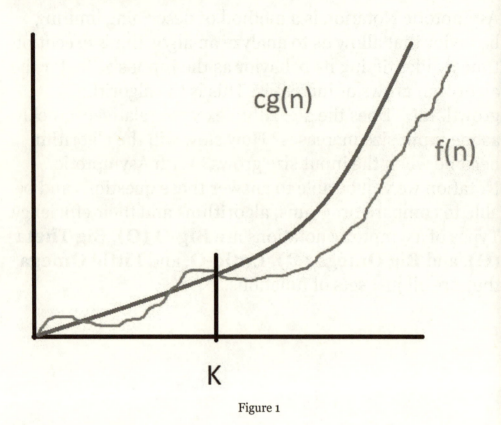

Figure 1

Big-O, which is usually written as O, is an Asymptotic Notation for the worst case, which is also the ceiling of growth for a given function. It provides us with what is called an ***asymptotic upper bound*** for the growth rate of the runtime of an algorithm.

Suppose $f(n)$ is your algorithm runtime, and $g(n)$ is an arbitrary time complexity you are trying to relate to your algorithm. $f(n)$ is $O(g(n))$, if $f(n) \leq c * g(n)$ whenever n ≥ k, where 'c' is some positive constant, and k ≥ 1.

Basically, the function f(n) is bounded by or won't go above some function c*g(n) after some input value we call 'k', like the graph above in Figure 1, and O(g(n)) is a set of functions of g(n). Let us look at an example by proving or showing that 2n + 1 belongs to O(n), which is sometimes written as 2n + 1= O(n).

Big-O Example:
Prove 2n + 1 = O(n)

Our functions are f(n) and g(n).
f(n) = 2n+1
g(n) = n

We want to show that there exist positive constants 'C' and 'K' such that
2n + 1 ≤ C * n whenever n ≥ K

We can guess a positive constant 'C' and 'K' that would satisfy this equation, I will show how to find a constant 'C' if 'K' is equal to 1.

1. Choose K=1 (1 is a positive constant)
2. Use algebra to solve for C

   $2n + 1 \leq Cn$, whenever $n \geq 1$

   $= 1 \leq Cn - 2n$, whenever $n \geq 1$

   $= 1 \leq n(C-2)$, whenever $n \geq 1$

   $= 1/n \leq C-2$, whenever $n \geq 1$

   $= 1/n + 2 \leq C$, whenever $n \geq 1$,

   Note: $1/n$ maximum value = 1, because $1/1 = 1$, and as n increases the value ($1/n$) decreases. For example, ½, and ¼, are all less than $1/1$. We can replace ($1/n$) with its maximum value (1) to get the following.

   $= 1 + 2 \leq C$

   $= 3 \leq C$

   This means we can choose a value for C that is equal to 3 or higher. Choose C=3 or higher.

3. We have now proven f(n) = 2n + 1, is O(n), since 2n+1 is always less than or equal to 3*n for all values of n greater than or equal to 1 and all values of C ≥ 3.

Big Omega Ω

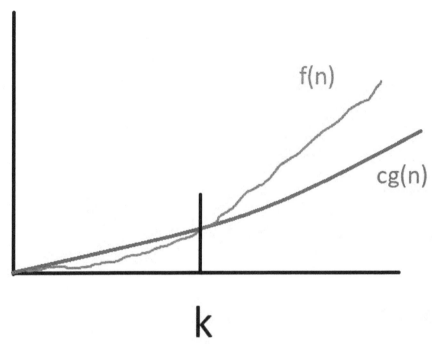

Figure 2

Big-Omega, which is usually written as **Ω**, is an Asymptotic Notation for the best case, which is also a floor growth rate for a given function. It provides us with an ***asymptotic lower bound*** for the growth rate of runtime of an algorithm.

f(n) belongs to $\Omega(g(n))$, if f(n) is $\geq$ c *g(n) whenever input size $n \geq k$, where 'c' is some positive constant, and k ≥ 1.

Basically, the function f(n) is bounded by or won't go below some function c*g(n) after some input value we call 'k', like the graph above in Figure 2, and Ω (g(n)) is a set of functions of g(n). Let us look at an example by proving or showing that 2n + 1 belongs to Ω (n), which is sometimes written as 2n + 1= Ω (n).

Big Omega Example:
Prove 2n + 1 = Ω (n)

Our functions are f(n) and g(n).
f(n) = 2n+1
g(n) = n

We want to show that there exist positive constants 'C' and 'K' such that
2n + 1 $\geq$ C * n whenever $n \geq$ K

We can guess a positive constant 'C' and 'K' that would satisfy this equation, I will show how to find a constant 'C' if 'K' is equal to 1.

1. Choose K=1 (1 is a positive constant)
2. Use algebra to solve for C

$2n + 1 \geq Cn$, whenever $n \geq 1$

$= 1 \geq Cn - 2n$, whenever $n \geq 1$

$= 1 \geq n(C-2)$, whenever $n \geq 1$

$= 1/n \geq C-2$, whenever $n \geq 1$

$= 1/n + 2 \geq C$, whenever $n \geq 1$,

Note: $1/n$ maximum value $= 1$, because $1/1 = 1$, and as n increases the value $(1/n)$ decreases. For example, ½, and ¼, are all less than $1/1$. We can replace $(1/n)$ with its maximum value (1) to get the following.

$= 1 + 2 \geq C$

$= 3 \geq C$

This means we can choose a value for C that is equal to 3 or lower. Choose C=3 or lower.

We have now proven $f(n) = 2n + 1$, is $\Omega(n)$, since 2n+1 is always greater than or equal to 3*n for all values of n greater than or equal to 1, and all values of $C \leq 3$.

Yes, a function can be Big O and Big Omega of the same function, which means that it is also Big Theta of the same function. This brings us to our third asymptotic Big Theta!

Big Theta Θ

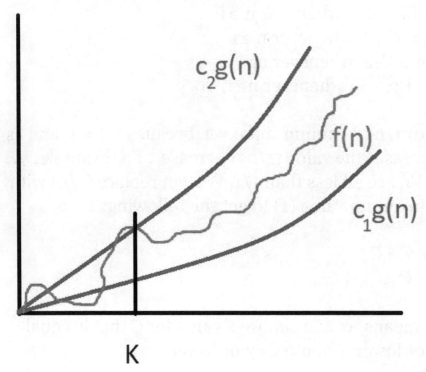

Figure 3

Big Theta or just Theta, which is usually written as **Θ**, is an Asymptotic Notation to denote the ***asymptotically tight bound*** on the growth rate of runtime of an algorithm.

f(n) is Θ(g(n)), if c1 * g(n) is ≤ f(n) and f(n) ≤ c2 *g(n) whenever n ≥ k for some positive constants c1, c2 and k,

$\therefore$ f(n) is $\Theta(g(n))$ implies f(n) is $O(g(n))$ and f(n) is $\Omega(g(n))$.

So, to show a function $f(n)$ is $\Theta(g(n))$ we must show a positive constant 'C' and 'K' that makes the above equations true.

Big Theta Example:

Prove that $2n + 1 = \Theta(n)$

We have already proven this from the previous two examples. All we must do is choose $C_1=3$, $C_2=3$, and $k=1$. Those values will satisfy the equation and make it true. However, note that c_1 could be less than 3, and c_2 could be greater than 3.

Little O– (o)

Little-O, which is usually written as **o**, provides us with what is called an ***asymptotic loose upper bound*** for the growth rate of the runtime of an algorithm. The main difference between little – o and big-o is the inequality sign.

Suppose $f(n)$ is your algorithm runtime, and $g(n)$ is an arbitrary time complexity you are trying to relate to your algorithm. $f(n)$ is o(g(n)) if $f(n)$ < $c * g(n)$ whenever n ≥ k, where 'c' is some positive constant, and k ≥ 1.

We say that f(n) is o(g(n)) if for **any real** constant c > 0, there exists an integer constant k ≥ 1 such that 0 ≤ f(n) < cg(n) for all n ≥ k. This means for any 'c' we must be able to find a 'k' that makes f(n) < c * g(n) asymptotically true.

Fun fact if you can prove a function is little-o of some function, then you have disproven that the function is Big Omega of the same function.

Little - o Example:

Prove 2n does not belong to $\Omega(n^2)$.

To prove this all we need to do is prove or show that 2n belongs to $o(n^2)$.

Our functions are f(n) and g(n).
f(n) = 2n
g(n) = n²

We must show for any 'C' we must be able to find a 'K' that makes f(n) < C * g(n) asymptotically true

1. Use algebra to solve the inequality
   2n < C * n², whenever n ≥ K
   = 2n/ n² < C, whenever n ≥ K
   = 2/n < C, whenever n ≥ K

Note: No matter what the constant value 'C' is we can come up with some value for 'K' that would make 2/n smaller since n ≥ K. As 'n' increases, 2/n decreases.

Therefore, we have proven 2n does not belong to $\Omega(n^2)$.

Little Omega - (ω)

Little Omega, which is usually written as **ω**, provides us with an ***asymptotic loose lower bound*** for the growth rate of runtime of an algorithm. The main difference between little – omega and big-omega is the inequality sign.

f(n) belongs to ω(g(n)) if, f(n) is > c *g(n) whenever input size n ≥ k, where 'c' is some positive constant, and k ≥ 1.

We say that f(n) is ω (g(n)) if for **any real** constant c > 0, there exists an integer constant k ≥ 1 such that 0 ≤ f(n) > cg(n) for all n ≥ k. This means for any 'c' we must be able to find a 'k' that makes f(n) > c * g(n) asymptotically true.

Fun fact if you can prove a function is little-omega of some function, then you have disproven that the function is Big-O of the same function.

Little Omega Example:

Prove 2^{2n} does not belong to $O(2^n)$.

To prove this all we need to do is prove or show that 2^{2n} belongs to $\omega(2^n)$.

Our functions are f(n) and g(n).
$f(n) = 2^{2n}$
$g(n) = 2^n$

We must show for any 'C' we must be able to find a 'K' that makes f(n) > C * g(n) asymptotically true

1. Use algebra to solve the inequality
    $2^{2n} > C*(2^n)$, whenever $n \geq K$
    $= (2^n)^2 > C*(2^n)$, whenever $n \geq K$
    $= (2^n)(2^n) > C*(2^n)$, whenever $n \geq K$
    $= (2^n) > C*1$, whenever $n \geq K$
    $= (2^n) > C$, whenever $n \geq K$

Note: The function 2^n will always grow faster than some constant value 'C'. For example, if we let C = 50, then no matter how 'n' increases, C will always be the value 50. For our function $f(n) = 2^n$, if K=10 then 'n' starts at 10, and our function equals $2^{10} = 1024$, and as 'n' increases f(n) increases.

We've now proven $f(n) = 2^{2n}$, is $\omega(n)$, since 2^{2n} is greater than some constant 'C' for all values of n greater than or equal to K. By doing so we have also proven that 2^{2n} does not belong to $O(2^n)$.

Omitting Bases in Logs in Asymptotic

For any logarithm function the base doesn't matter, we simply state it's $\Theta(\log n)$. For example, $\log_2(n)$ belongs to $\Theta(\log n)$, as well as $\log_5(n)$ or $\log_{10}(n)$ and so on. Let's do a proof to show why we do not consider base of log in time complexity.

Example:

Let's look at the definition of Big O. A function $f(n)$ is said to belong to $O(g(n))$ if and only if $f(n) \leq C^*g(n)$ whenever n $\geq$K, where both K and C are constants.

We want to show $\log_a(n)$ is $O(\log_b(n))$, where constants a>1, and b>1. This means a and b can be any constant value greater than 1.

Our functions are f(n) and g(n).
$f(n) = \log_a(n)$
$g(n) = \log_b(n)$

We want to show that there exist positive constants 'C' and 'K' such that
$\log_a(n) \leq C * \log_b(n)$ whenever $n \geq K$

We can guess a positive constant 'C' and 'K' that would satisfy this equation.

1. Choose K=1 (1 is a positive constant)
2. Choose $C = \log_a(b)$
3. Use algebra to solve for C
$= \log_a(n) \leq \log_a(b) * \log_b(n)$ whenever $n \geq 1$
$= \log_a(n) \leq \log_b(n) * \log_a(b)$ whenever $n \geq 1$
$= \log_a(n) \leq \log_a(b^{\log_b(n)})$ whenever $n \geq 1$
$= \log_a(n) \leq \log_a(n)$ whenever $n \geq 1$

Note: This equation is always true no matter what the value of n is, therefore the base of logarithms do not matter. We can do the same for Big Omega, which implies we can do this proof for Big Theta.

Chapter 3:
Growth & analysis of functions

3.1 Orders of growth:

An algorithm can show a rate of growth on the order of some mathematical function. **Order of growth** for an algorithm shows how the resource (space, time, or energy) for computation increases when you increase the input size 'n'. It matters a lot when your input size is extremely large. This provides only a crude description of the behavior of a process.

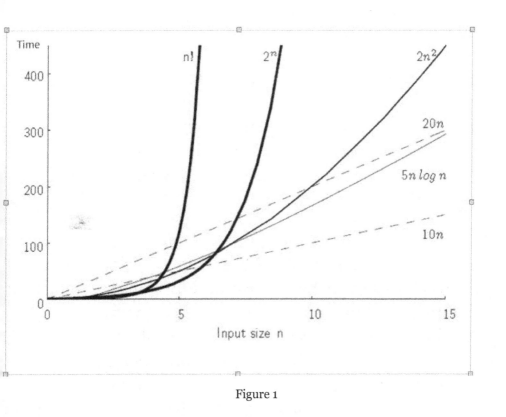

Figure 1

Notice the graph above (Figure 1), there are many functions, and as the input size 'n' increases on the X-axis, the functions time increases differently on the Y-axis. For example, n factorial (n!) time is 400 unit of time when n=5, while the function 10*n is only 50 unit of time when n=5.

Let's look at some functions growth classifications below, their growth is ordered from slowest growing function to the fastest growing functions.

1. Constant Function: $f(n) = c$, where 'c' is a constant value.
2. Logarithmic Function: $f(n) = \log n$
3. Quadratic Function: $f(n) = an^2 + bn + c$
4. Polynomial Function: $f(n) = an^k + ...$ $+an^2+an^1+an^0$, where k is some constant.
5. Exponential Function: $f(n) = c^n$, where c is some constant

When it comes to asymptotic notation, the higher function is always taken over the lower function. For example, if we had a function like $f(n) = 5n^2 + (n!)$, then the function would be $\Theta(n!)$. We can see from the graph above (Figure 1) that n! grows faster than a quadratic function like n^2, as a matter of fact it grows faster than an exponential function. Another example would be $f(n) = 10n + 2n^2$, then our function f(n) belongs to $\Theta(n^2)$, because $2n^2$ grows faster than 10n.

3.2 Analyzing Sets of Faster Growing Functions:

The sets below take the fastest growing function.

Constant Functions
$\Theta(1) + \Theta(1) + \Theta(1) = \Theta(1)$
$\Theta(1) + \Theta(1000) = \Theta(1)$
$\Theta(1) + \Theta(C) = \Theta(1)$, where C is some positive constant

Logarithmic Functions
$\Theta(logn) + \Theta(logn) = \Theta(logn)$
$\Theta(logn) + \Theta(\text{log with any constant base}) = \Theta(logn)$

Linear Functions
$\Theta(n) + \Theta(n) = \Theta(n)$
$\Theta(n) + \Theta(An+B) = \Theta(n)$, where A & B are positive constants

Linearithmic Functions
$\Theta(nlogn) + \Theta(nlogn) = \Theta(nlogn)$
$\Theta(nlogn) + \Theta(n * \text{log with any constant base}) = \Theta(nlogn)$

Quadratic Functions
$\Theta(n^2) + \Theta(n^2) = \Theta(n^2)$
$\Theta(n^2) + \Theta(An^2+B+C) = \Theta(n^2)$, where A,B & C are positive

Some Extra Sets Using Asymptotic Notation
$\Theta(1) + \Theta(n) = \Theta(n)$
$\Theta(1) + \Theta(1) + \Theta(n) + \Theta(n) = \Theta(n)$
$\Theta(n^2) + \Theta(n) + \Theta(1) = \Theta(n^2)$
$\Theta(1) + \Theta(2) + \Theta(n * \log n) + \Theta(n^2) + \Theta(\log n) +$
$\Theta(n!) = \Theta(n!)$

Chapter 4:
Analysis of programs & algorithms

4.1 Analysis Types

The algorithm complexity can be best, average or worst-case analysis. The algorithm analysis can be expressed using Big O notation. Best, worst, and average cases of a given algorithm express what the resource usage is at least, at most and on average, respectively. The Big O notation simplifies the comparison of algorithms.

Best Case

Best case performance used in computer science to describe an algorithm's behavior under optimal conditions. An example of best case performance would be trying to sort a list that is already sorted using some sorting algorithm. E.G. [1,2,3] --> [1,2,3]

Average Case

Average case performance measured using the average optimal conditions to solve the problem. For example, a list that is neither best case nor, worst case order that you want to be sorted in a certain order. E.G. [2,1,5,3] --> [1,2,3,5] OR [2,1,5,3] --> [5,3,2,1]

Worst Case

Worst case performance used to analyze the algorithm's behavior under worst case input and least possible to solve the problem. It determines when the algorithm will perform worst for the given inputs. An example of the worst-case performance would be a list of names already sorted in ascending order that you want to sort in descending order. E.G. [Abby, Bill, Catherine] --> [Catherine, Bill, Abby].

4.2 Understanding Code Complexity

The algorithm complexity ignores the constant value in algorithm analysis and takes only the highest order. Suppose we had an algorithm that takes, $5n^3+n+4$ time to calculate all the steps, then the algorithm analysis ignores all the lower order polynomials and constants and takes only $O(n^3)$. Let us look at some common running times and source code snippets below.

Simple Statement

This statement takes some constant amount of time, so it is **O (1)** time.

1. int y = n + 25;

For / While Loops

If the for loop takes n times to complete then it is **O(n)**.

```
1. for (int i=0; i<n; i++){
2.  //Some constant work
3. }
```

We can write or represent a loop as a summation, to solve the number of iterations that occur within in it. Basically, we are trying to solve the number of times the statement within the loop is being executed. A summation representation of the for loop above is below, where c is some constant value:

$$\sum_{i=0}^{n-1} constant\ work$$

$$\sum_{i=0}^{n-1} c$$

Note that the summation above starts at i=0 and runs until "i" reaches "n-1". The summation stops at n-1 instead of "n" because the loop runs while "i < n" so "i" never reaches "n" it stops 1 iteration before this means "i < n" is equivalent to "i ≤ n-1". Let's solve the summation above:

$$\sum_{i=0}^{n-1} c = c \sum_{i=0}^{n-1} 1 = c * n = O(n)$$

After solving the summation, we can see that it is Big -O of "n", since c*n is O(n) for all values of c > 0.

The following **while** loop takes n time as well to complete and so it is **O(n)**.

1. int i=0;
2. while (i<n){
3.   //Some constant work
4.   i++;
5. }

If the **for** loop takes n time and i increases or decreases by a constant, the cost is **O(n)**.

1. for(int i=0; i<n; i+=5)
2.   sum++; //A constant amount of work

1. for(int i=n; i>0; i-=5)
2.   sum++; //A constant amount of work

Let's see what the for loop below would look like as represented by a summation and solve its running time, the number of times sum++ is being executed:

1. for(int i=0; i<n; i+=5)

2.   sum++; //A constant amount of work

$$\sum_{i=0}^{\frac{n}{5}-1} c = c \sum_{i=0}^{\frac{n}{5}-1} 1 = c * (n/5) = O(n)$$

As you can see we simply divided n by 5, because i increases by 5. To make this more obvious let's suppose we had the same for loop, "for(int i=0; i<n; i+=5){sum++}". We can see that if n=10, then the loop would run as follows:

i=0, check if 0<10 it is so continue the loop
i=5, check if 5 < 10 it is so continue the loop
i=10, check if 10 < 10 it is not stop the loop

So, we can see that the loop ran only 2 times, the third time it checks if i<10, which it isn't so it stops. In general, a summation in the form "**for(int i=0; i<n; i+=a){sum++}**", where 'a' is some constant, then the summation is:

$$\sum_{i=0}^{\frac{n}{a}-1} c = c\sum_{i=0}^{\frac{n}{a}-1} 1 = c * (n/a) = O(n)$$

If the **for** loop takes n time and i increases or decreases by a multiple, the cost is **O(log(n))**

1. for(int i=1; i<=n; i*=2)
2.   sum++; //A constant amount of work

1. for(int i=n; i>0; i/=2)
2.   sum++; //A constant amount of work

Let's see what the for loop below would look like as represented by a summation and solve its running time, the number of times sum++ is being executed:

1. for(int i=1; i<=n; i*=2)
2.   sum++; //A constant amount of work

$$\sum_{i=1}^{\log n+1} c = c \sum_{i=1}^{\log n+1} 1 = c * \log n + 1 = O(\log n)$$

NOTE: log n is $\log_2 n$.

Nested Loops

If the nested loops contain sizes n and m, the cost is **O(nm)**

1. for(int i=0; i < n; i++)

2.   for(int j=0; j < m; j++)

3.   sum ++;

Let's see what the for loop above would look like as represented by a summation and solve its running time, the number of times sum++ is being executed:

$$\sum_{i=0}^{n-1} \left(\sum_{j=0}^{m-1} c \right) = c \sum_{i=0}^{n-1} m = c * m * \sum_{i=0}^{n-1} 1 = c * m * n = O(mn)$$

If the first loop runs N times and the inner loop runs log(n) times or (vice versa), the cost is **O(n*log(n))**

1. for(int i=0; i < n; i++)

2.   for(int j=1; j <= n; j*=4)

3.   sum ++;

Let's see what the for loop above would look like as represented by a summation and solve its running time, the number of times sum++ is being executed:

$$\sum_{i=0}^{n-1}\left(\sum_{j=1}^{\log n+1} c\right) = c \sum_{i=0}^{n-1}\left(\sum_{j=1}^{\log n+1} 1\right)$$

$$= c \sum_{i=0}^{n-1} \log n + 1 = c * (\log n + 1) * \sum_{i=0}^{n-1} 1$$

$$= c * (\log n + 1) * n = O(n * \log n)$$

If the inner loop runs n^2 times and the first loop runs n times or (vice versa), the cost is **O(n^3)**

1. for(int i=0; i < n; i++)

2.   for(int j=0; j < n *n; j++)

3.   sum ++;

Let's see what the for loop above would look like as represented by a summation and solve its running time, the number of times sum++ is being executed:

$$\sum_{i=0}^{n-1}\left(\sum_{j=0}^{n*n-1} c\right) = c \sum_{i=0}^{n-1} n * n$$

$$= c * n * n * \sum_{i=0}^{n-1} 1 = c * n * n * n = O(n\text{^}3)$$

If the first loop runs n times and the inner second loop runs n^2 times and the third loop runs n^2, then **O(n^5)**

1. for(int i=0; i < n; i++)

2.   for(int j=0; j < n * n; j++)

3.   for(int k=0; k <j; k++)

4.   sum ++;

Let's see what the for loop above would look like as represented by a summation:

$$\sum_{i=0}^{n-1}\sum_{j=0}^{n*n-1}\sum_{k=0}^{j-1} c$$

Now let us look at some trickier code snippets and determine the runtime in terms of Big O.

O(1)

Your initial thoughts for this code snippet may be that it should be **O(n),** but it will only check if "j<n" once and find that n is not less than n, so this runs a constant amount of time.

```
for(int j=n; j<n; j++)
sum ++;
```

O(1)

Your initial thoughts for this code snippet may be that it should be O(log n), but notice that the for loop starts j at '0' so it will never be greater than 'n', hence it runs a constant amount of time. Wait, but what if n is a negative number, well according to the definition of Big -O, n must be positive.

```
for(int j=0; j>n; j*=2)
    sum++;
```

O(n)

Your initial thoughts for this code snippet might be O(n * log(n)), but this is actually O(n).

```
for(int i=n; i>0; i/=2)
  for(int j=0; j<i; j++)
    count++;
```

or

```
for(int i=1; i<n; i*=2)
  for(int j=0; j<i; j++)
    count++;
```

The latter loop as a summation, where log n = $\log_2 n$ rounded up.

$$\sum_{i=1}^{\log n} \sum_{j=0}^{2^{(i-1)}} c = c \sum_{i=0}^{\log n} 2^{i-1} = c(2^{(\log n)} - 1) = c(n - 1)$$

Note: c(n-1) = O(n)

O(n⁴)

This code below looks crazy, and you may think the running time of this code is **O(n³)** because of the three for loops, however it is **O(n⁴).** Notice the first loop runs n*n times which is O(n²), the second loop runs i times , and i runs O(n²) times, the last loop runs 6 times or O(1). So we get O(n²) * O(n²) * O(1) , which is O(n⁴).

```
for(int i=1; i<n*n; i++)
   for(int j=1; j≤i; j++)
      for(int k=1; k≤ 6; k++)
         sum ++;
```

4.3 Analyze Selection Sort Algorithm

Alg.: SELECTION-SORT(A)		
	cost	Times
n ← length[A]	c_1	1
for j ← 1 to n - 1	c_2	n-1
do smallest ← j	c_3	n-1
for i ← j + 1 to n	c_4	$\sum_{j=1}^{n-1}(n-j+1)$
≈ n2/2 comparisons, do if A[i]<A[smallest]	c_5	$\sum_{j=1}^{n-1}(n-j)$
then smallest ← i	c_6	$\sum_{j=1}^{n-1}(n-j)$
≈ n exchanges, exchange A[j] ↔ A[smallest]	c_7	n-1

OVERVIEW

Selection sort is a sorting algorithm in computer science. It has $O(n^2)$ time complexity. $O(n^2)$ isn't a good time complexity for sorting lists when it comes to large input sizes. This algorithm sorts an array or list by repeatedly finding the minimum value (if we are sorting in ascending order) from the list or array and placing it at the beginning of the list. Here I am going to go line by line on the selection sort algorithm to compute the algorithms runtime.

arr[] = 65 25 12 22 10

// Find the minimum element in arr[0...4]
// and place it at beginning
10 30 12 22 65

// Find the minimum element in arr[1...4]
// and place it at beginning of arr[1...4]
10 12 30 22 65

// Find the minimum element in arr[2...4]
// and place it at beginning of arr[2...4]
10 12 22 30 65

// Find the minimum element in arr[3...4]
// and place it at beginning of arr[3...4]
10 12 22 30 65

Selection Sort C-Program Analysis

Here I am going to analyze the code being executed line by line (this does not include comments). There are two things we need to keep track of to analyze the time complexity of the selection sort algorithm and that is the cost it takes to execute the statement at each line and the number of times the statement at that line is executed.

```c
// C program for implementation of selection sort
//NOTE: REMOVE The Line Numbers (e.g. Line 1.) if you want to run this code
// I inserted them to help with the analysis
#include <stdio.h>
void selectionSort(int arr[], int n)
{
 Line 1.int i, j, min_idx;

  // One by one move boundary of unsorted subarray
 Line 2. for (i = 0; i < n; i++){
// Find the minimum element in unsorted array
 Line 3.   min_idx = i;
 Line 4. for (j = i+1; j < n; j++){
 Line 5.     if (arr[j] < arr[min_idx])
 Line 6.       min_idx = j;}
// Swap the found minimum element with the first element
 Line 7.   int temp = arr[min_dx];
 Line 8.   arr[min_dx] = arr[i];
 Line 9.   arr[i] = temp;
  }
}
/* Function to print an array */
void printArray(int arr[], int size){
 int i;
 for (i=0; i < size; i++)
   printf("%d ", arr[i]);
 printf("\n");
}
// Driver program to test above functions
int main(){
 int arr[] = {64, 25, 12, 22, 11};
 int n = sizeof(arr)/sizeof(arr[0]);
 selectionSort(arr, n);
 printf("Sorted array: \n");
 printArray(arr, n);
 return 0;
}
```

Inside the Selection Sort Function:

Line 1: **COST**= C1, **TIME** = 1, where C1 is some constant

Line 2: **COST**=C2, **TIME** = n+1, where C2 is some constant

Line 3: **COST** = C3, **TIME** = n, where C3 is some constant

Line 4: **COST** = C4, **TIME** = (n²-n) / 2 + n, where C4 is some constant

Line 5: **COST** = C5, **TIME** = $(n^2-n) / 2$, where C5 is some constant
Line 6: **COST**= C6, **TIME** = $(n^2-n) / 2$, where C6 is some constant
Line 7: **COST** = C7, **TIME** = n, where C7 is some constant
Line 8: **COST** = C8, **TIME** = n, where C8 is some constant
Line 9: **COST** = C9, **TIME** = n, where C9 is some constant

Now that we have all the costs and the times, we must sum up all the costs times the time to get the runtime:

Runtime = $(C1 *1) + (C2 *(n+1)) + (C3 *n) + (C4 * ((n^2-n)/2) + n) + (C5 * (n^2-n) / 2) + (C6 * (n^2-n) / 2) + (C7 * n) + (C8 * n)+ (C9 * n)$

U = C1 + C2
V= C2 + C3 -C4/2 + C4-C5/2-C6/2+C7+C8+ C9
W = C4/2 + C5 /2+C6

Where U, V, and W are constants
= $U +Vn + Wn^2$
= $O(n^2)$

4.4 Analyze Bubble Sort Algorithm

Bubble Sort Overview

Bubble Sort is considered one of the simplest sorting algorithms that works by repeatedly swapping the adjacent elements if they are in the wrong order. With a bubble sort algorithm, you will be able to see that the largest element (assuming we are sorting from smallest to largest) will "*bubble*" up to the top of the list or array.

The procedure or algorithm that we will use is below:

This algorithm uses a flag to tell if the elements have been swapped or not, which allows the bubble sort algorithm best case to be **O(n)** instead of **O(n²)** like another implementation of bubble sort.

```
procedure bubbleSort(A : list of sortable items )
    n = length(A)
    repeat
        swapped = false
        for i = 1 to n-1 inclusive do
            /* if this pair is out of order */
            if A[i-1] > A[i] then
                /* swap them and remember something changed */
                swap(A[i-1], A[i])
                swapped = true
            end if
        end for
    until not swapped
end procedure
```

Example: Suppose we want to sort a list or array of elements in ascending order (from smallest to largest): List = **(3,1,2)**. *Note that this is the Average Case.*

Average Case

First Pass:

(3,1,2) -> Here the algorithm compares the first two elements (3 & 1)

(1,3,2) -> Here the algorithm swaps 1 and 3 since 1 < 3

(1,**3,2**) -> Here the algorithm compares the 2nd and 3rd

elements (3 & 2)

(1,**2,3**) -> Here the algorithm swaps 3 and 2since 2< 3

Second Pass:

(**1,2**,3) -> Here the algorithm compares the first two elements (1 & 2)

(1,2,3) -> No SWAPPING, because 1 < 2

(1,**2,3**) -> Here the algorithm compares the 2nd and 3rd elements (2 & 3)

(1,2,3) -> No SWAPPING, because 2< 3

Since no swapping occurred, this tells us that the array is already sorted in ascending order!

Best Case

Now let's try this same algorithm again but this time using the best-case scenario, which is when the elements are already sorted in the order (ascending) we would like.

(**1,2**,3) -> Here the algorithm compares the first two elements (1 & 2)

(**1**,2,3) -> No SWAPPING, because 1 < 2

(1,**2,3**) -> Here the algorithm compares the 2nd and 3rd elements (2 & 3)

(1,**2,3**) -> No SWAPPING, because 2< 3

Since no swapping occurred we are done, and the algorithm only did 2 comparisons and the number of elements in the array we will call n=3. So, we can see that for n elements this algorithm best case will take only n-1 comparisons, **n-1 = O(n)**

Let's look at a different implementation of the bubble sort algorithm:

```
BUBBLESORT(A)
1 for i = 1 to A.length - 1
2     for j = A.length downto i + 1
3         if A[j] < A[j - 1]
4             exchange A[j] with A[j - 1]
```

The above algorithm Worst *Case = O(n²)* and *Best Case = O(n²)*

Worst Case

Let's sort an array or list = (3,2,1) this would be the ***worst case*** where the list is in the complete opposite order than that we wish (in ascending order) using the above algorithm.

First Pass: (**3,2**,1) -> Compare the elements 3 & 2 (**2,3**,1) -> Swap 3 & 2 since 2 < 3 (2,**3,1**) -> Compare the elements 3 & 1 (2,**1,3**) -> Swap 1 & 3 since 1 < 3

Second Pass: (2,1,3) -> Compare the elements 2 & 1 (**1,2**,3) -> Swap 2 & 1 since 1 < 2 (1,**2,3**) -> Compare the elements 2 & 3 (1,**2,3**) -> No SWAPPING needed since 2 < 3

We have now finished looping through both loops, so the array must be sorted in ascending order.

Notice we made 4 comparisons in the above second example, and the number of elements in the array we will call 'n' = 3, so the number of comparisons made is $(n-1)^2$, and $(n-1)^2 = \mathbf{O(n^2)}$

C-Program of the Bubble Sort Algorithm is below:

/*This program sorts an array of elements using the bubble sort algorithm

Output:
Enter total number(s) of elements: 4
Enter the 4 elements: 1 5 4 3
After Sorting: 1 3 4 5 */

```c
#include <stdio.h>

int BubbleSort(int size, int *array);

int main(void){

        int size, i, array[20];

        printf("Enter total number(s) of elements: ");
        scanf("%d", &size);

        printf("Enter the %d elements: ", size);
        for(i=0; i<size; i++){
                scanf("%d", &array[i]);
        }

        //Run the Bubble Sort Algorithm to sort the list of elements
        BubbleSort(size, array);

        printf("After Sorting: ");
        for(i=0; i<size; i++){
                printf(" %d", array[i]);
        }

        printf("\n");
        system("pause"); // comment this line if you are not using Windows OS
        return 0;
}

int BubbleSort(int size, int *array){

        int i, j, temp;

        //Bubble sorting algorthm
        for(i=size-2; i>= 0; i--){
                for(j=0; j<=i; j++){

                        //Swap
                        if(array[j] > array[j+1]){
                                temp = array[j];
                                array[j] = array[j+1];
                                array[j+1]= temp;
                        }
                }
        }

        return 1;
}
```

Useful Summation Formulas & Properties:

Summations Formulas Description

Here are some of the most commonly used formulas for summations used in computer science.

$$\sum_{i=1}^{n} c = c + c + c + \ldots + c$$

$$\sum_{i=m}^{n} 1 = n + 1 - m$$

$$\sum_{i=m}^{n} i = \frac{n(n+1)}{2} - \frac{m(m-1)}{2} = \frac{(n+1-m)(n+m)}{2}$$

$$\sum_{i=0}^{n} i = \sum_{i=1}^{n} i = \frac{n(n+1)}{2}$$

$$\sum_{i=0}^{n} i^2 = \frac{n(n+1)(2n+1)}{6} = \frac{n^3}{3} + \frac{n^2}{2} + \frac{n}{6}$$

$$\sum_{i=0}^{n} i^3 = \left(\frac{n(n+1)}{2}\right)^2 = \frac{n^4}{4} + \frac{n^3}{2} + \frac{n^2}{4} = \left[\sum_{i=1}^{n} i\right]^2$$

Summation manipulation properties:

$$\sum_{n=s}^{t} C \cdot f(n) = C \cdot \sum_{n=s}^{t} f(n)$$

$$\sum_{n=s}^{t} f(n) + \sum_{n=s}^{t} g(n) = \sum_{n=s}^{t} [f(n) + g(n)]$$

$$\sum_{n=s}^{t} f(n) - \sum_{n=s}^{t} g(n) = \sum_{n=s}^{t} [f(n) - g(n)]$$

$$\sum_{n=s}^{t} f(n) = \sum_{n=s+p}^{t+p} f(n-p)$$

$$\sum_{n=s}^{j} f(n) + \sum_{n=j+1}^{t} f(n) = \sum_{n=s}^{t} f(n)$$

$$\sum_{i=k_0}^{k_1} \sum_{j=l_0}^{l_1} a_{i,j} = \sum_{j=l_0}^{l_1} \sum_{i=k_0}^{k_1} a_{i,j}$$

$$\sum_{n=0}^{t} f(2n) + \sum_{n=0}^{t} f(2n+1) = \sum_{n=0}^{2t+1} f(n)$$

$$\sum_{n=s}^{t} \ln f(n) = \ln \prod_{n=s}^{t} f(n)$$

Chapter 5:
Analyzing recursive algorithms

5.1 Recursion

Recursion in computer science is a method where the solution to a problem depends on solutions to smaller instances of the same problem (as opposed to iteration). Recursive algorithms have two cases: a recursive case and base case. Any function that calls itself is recursive. Examples of recursive functions:

1. Factorial: n! = n x (n -1) x (n-2) x ... x 1

2. Fibonacci: 1,1,2,3,5,8, ...

3. Multiplication (3 x 2): 3 + 3

4. Multiplication (2 x 3): 2 + 2 + 2

5. $\sum_{i=1}^{5} i$ = 1 + 2 + 3 + 4 + 5

6. n^2 + $(n-1)^2$ + $(n-2)^2$ + ... + 1

7. 1 + 10 + 100 + 1000 + 10000 + ...

8. 1 + 1 + 1 + ... + 1

9. 0 + 1 + 2 + 3 + ... + n

10. func(0) = 0 , func(n) = func(n-1) + n

11. A Mandelbrot Set

Recursion is useful for tasks that can be defined in terms of similar subtasks, for example search, sort, and traversal problems often have simple recursive solutions. At some point the function encounters a subtask that it can perform without calling itself.

• **Directly recursive:** method that calls itself

• **Indirectly recursive:** method that calls another method and eventually results in the original method call

• **Tail recursive method:** recursive method in which the last statement executed is the recursive call

• **Infinite recursion:** case where every recursive call result in another recursive call

Recursion Function to Multiply Two Numbers

Multiplication can be thought of as a recursive function. Multiplication is simply adding the number 'X' 'Y' times or vice versa. For example, if I multiplied 5 by 3 (e.g. 5 * 3) the way multiplication works, we get 5 + 5 + 5 = 15 or 3 + 3 +3+ 3+ 3= 15 both are correct ways to do multiplication. This works perfectly for positive integers, but what if we wanted to multiply 5 * 0 = 0 or 0 * 5 =0 and 5 * 1 = 5 or 1 * 5 = 5, that will be our base case also known as the stopping or non-recursive case.

So, what will the recursive program look like? For the base case if input X or input Y is 0, then we will return 0, if X is 1 then we return Y, if Y is 1 then we return X. Both X and Y are our input parameter variables. The recursive multiplication function is below to multiply two positive numbers recursively. Note: you cannot use this function for negative values.

```
int Multiply(int X, int Y){
if( X == 0 || Y== 0)
return 0;

if(X == 1)
return Y;

if(Y == 1)
return X;

returnY + Multiply(X -1, Y);
}
```

Fibonacci Recursive Function

The Fibonacci sequence is named after the Italian mathematician Leonardo of Pisa also known as Fibonacci. Although the sequence was described earlier in Indian mathematics, he introduced it to the Western European mathematics. The first two numbers of the infinite sequence are either 0 and 1 or 1 and 1, and every other preceding number is the sum of the two previous numbers.

Fibonacci Sequence: 1,1,2,3,5,8,13, 21,....
Modern Fibonacci Sequence: 0, 1, 1, 2, 3, 5, 8, 13, 21,...

The Fibonacci Sequence is defined by the following recurrence relation:

Fib(0) = 0

Fib(1) = 1

Fib(n) = Fib(n-1) + Fib(n-2)

Don't be over whelmed by the recurrence relation above. Fib(n) is just a function like f(x), Fib is short for Fibonacci. Fib(0) is a Fibonacci function with input 0, and outputs the value 0, and is considered one of the base cases because it returns a specific constant. Fib(1) is a Fibonacci function with input 1, and it outputs the value 1, it is another base case of the Fibonacci function. Now for the tricky part Fib(n) is the recursive case of the Fibonacci function with some arbitrary input 'n' it is equal to Fib(n-1) + Fib(n-2). Recursive just means it's a function that calls itself or is defined by itself. So, if for example n = 2, then the function would give us the following:

$Fib(2) = Fib(2-1) + Fib(2-2)$

$= Fib(1) + Fib(0)$

$= 1 + 0$

$= 1$

We see that given n=2, the recursive function gives us the value 1. So, the input of 'n' is the index of the Fibonacci number and the output is the number in the Fibonacci sequence. Let's look at an example.

Fibonacci Sequence: 0,1,1,2,3,5,8,13

Index of Sequence : 0,1,2,3,4,5,6

This means if we input the value n=0 we get the Fibonacci number 0, if we input the value n=6 into our algorithm, we get back the Fibonacci number 8. The running time or Time Complexity is $T(n) = O(1.6180)^n$, and it's recurrence relation is $T(n) = T(n-1) + T(n-2) + C$, where C is a constant.

Fun Fact:

1.6180 is also called the golden ratio, and it's appearance can be found throughout nature: face, body, flower petals, animals, Fibonacci series, shell, galaxies, arts, architecture etc.

C-Program for Fibonacci:

```c
/*
This program recurssively finds and prints the fibonacci number.
*/

# include<stdio.h>

int fib(int n);

int main(void)
{
        int i;
        int n;

        printf("Input the index of the fibinocci sequence\n");
        scanf("%d", &n);

        printf("\nThe first %d fibonacci series numbers\n", n);

        for(i=0; i<=n; i++)
        {
                printf("%d ", fib(i));
        }
        printf("\n\n");
        system("pause");
}

int fib(int n)
{
        if(n== 0)
          return 0;

        if(n==1)
          return 1;

          return fib(n-1) + fib(n-2);
}
```

Factorial Program

The Factorial Algorithm is great for recursion.

Factorial !

$1! = 1$

$2! = 2(1) = 2$

$3! = 3(2)(1) = 6$

What is factorial?

In mathematics, the factorial of a non-negative integer n, denoted by n!, is the product of all positive integers less than or equal to n. For example,
$5! = 5 \times 4 \times 3 \times 2 \times 1 = 120$. It is just the product of an integer and all the integers below it.

How to write a factorial function using recursion?

The factorial program can be written recursively because it is a function that calls itself.

Pseudo Code
1. *func factorial(n)*
2. *if (n == 1)*
3. *return 1*
4. *return n * factorial (n -1)*

This function written as a recurrence relation is:

$T(n)=1$ *for n=1*
$T(n)=1+T(n-1)$ *for n>0*

This recurrence running time in Big O notation is: **O(n)**, which is the main purpose for converting algorithms to recurrence relations.

Let's look at an example:
Suppose we had an arbitrary number n=5, so we use the function factorial (5).

We get the following Number of iterations
1) factorial(5) = 5 * factorial(4)
2) factorial(4) = 4 * factorial(3)
3) factorial(3) = 3 * factorial(2)
4) factorial(2) = 2 * factorial(1)
5) factorial(1) = 1

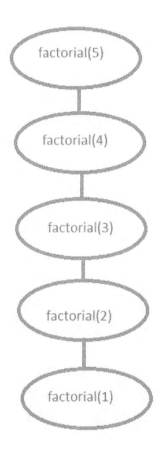

The recursion performed by the factorial function 5! takes only 5 steps. This means the factorial function is O(n) since our input size "n" = 5 and it took only 5 steps

So, the factorial function called itself 5 times which is the exact same number of the input size 'n', where n = 5. So, the recurrence ran 'n' times, and is therefore **O(n)**.

Factorial C Program

```
/*
This program outputs the factorial of a number e.g. 5! = 5 * 4 * 3 * 2 * 1 = 120.
In general n! = n * n-1 * n-2* ... * 3 * 2 * 1
*/

# include<stdio.h>

int fact_recursive(int n);// This is a recursive factorial function
int fact_iterative(int n);// This is a iterative factorial function

int main(void)
{
        int n;

        printf("Enter a number: ");
        scanf("%d", &n);

        printf("%d! = %d\n", n, fact_iterative(n));

        system("pause");
}

fact_recursive(int n)
{
        //Base Case
        if(n == 0)
        return 1;

        return n *fact_recursive(n-1);
}

int fact_iterative(int n)
{
        int i;
        int product = 1;
        for(i = 1; i<= n; i++)
        {
                product = product * i;
        }

        return product;
}
```

5.2 Recurrence Relation

What is a recurrence relation? "In mathematics, a **recurrence relation** is an equation that recursively defines a sequence or multidimensional array of values, once one or more initial terms are given: each further term of the sequence or array is defined as a function of the preceding terms."

Recurrence Relation Examples:
1. $T(n) = T(n/3) + 100, T(2) = 3$
2. $T(x) = T(x) + 1, T(1) = 1$
3. $A_n = A_{n-1} + 3, A_0 = 5$

Recurrence relations are used to determine the running time of recursive programs – recurrence relations themselves are recursive.

$T(0)$ = Time to solve problem of size 0
$T(n)$ = Time to solve problem of size n

5.3 How to Solve Recurrence Relation Running Time?

There are many ways to solve a recurrence relation running time:

(1) Master Theorem
(2) Substitution / Iteration
(3) Induction
(4) Change of Variance
(5) Recursion Tree
(6) Akra-Bazzi Method

Master Theorem

To solve a recurrence relation running time you can use many different techniques. One popular technique is to use the **Master Theorem** also known as the **Master Method**. The Master Theorem is a cookbook method to solve asymptotic terms for recurrence relations of a specific form. These recurrence relations are used for a lot of the divide and conquer algorithms. This method can only be used for equations in the form of $T(n) = AT(n/B) + \Theta(n^C)$, where $\Theta(n^C)$ is a function of n or equivalent f(n).

Given A Recurrence Equation in the form:
$T(n) = AT(n/B) + \Theta(n^C * \log n)$

Case 1 to solve the function running time:
If $C < \log_B A$ then $T(n) = \Theta(n^{\wedge}\log_B A)$

Case 2 to solve the function running time:
If $C = \log_B A$ then $T(n) = \Theta(n^C * \log^{k+1}(n))$, for $k > -1$

Case 3 to solve the function running time:
If $C > \log_B A$ then $T(n) = \Theta(n^C)$

Regularity condition: $Af(n/B) \leq C*f(n)$

Example: Solve the runtime of the following recurrence relation $T(n) = 3T(n/2) + n$

Note: $n = n^1$
A=3, B=2, C=1, k=0

 Next, we check the three cases, and since all three cases involve $\log_B A$ to be compared with C, we will go ahead and solve for that first. $\log_2 3 = 1.584963$.

So, C=1 and this is less than $\log_2 3 = 1.584963$, this means Case 1 is true.

Case 1 states: If $C < \log_B A$ then $T(n) = \Theta (n \char`\^ \log_B A) \rightarrow$ If $1 < 1.584963$ Then $T(n) = \Theta (n^{1.584963})$ $= \Theta (n^{\log(3)})$

Master Theorem Case 2 Extension

Given A Recurrence Equation in the form:
$$T(n) = AT(n/B) + \Theta(n^C * \log' n)$$

If $C = \log_B A$ then:

Case 1:
$T(n) = \Theta(n^C * \log^{k+1}(n))$, if $k > -1$

Case 2:
$T(n) = \Theta(n^C * \log \log(n))$, if $k = -1$

Case 1:
$T(n) = \Theta(n^C)$, if $k < -1$

Example: Solve the runtime of the following recurrence relation $T(n) = 4T(n/2) + n^2 / \ln(n)$

Note: $T(n) = 4T(n/2) + n^2 * \log^{-1}_e(n)$
$A=4$, $B=2$, $C=2$, $k=-1$

Next, we check if $\log_B A = C$, $\log_2 4 = 2 = C$.

Now we have everything we need to solve this recurrence relation. We will use Case 2! **Case 2** states: $T(n) = \Theta(n^C * \log \log(n))$ if $k = -1 \rightarrow$
$T(n) = \Theta(n^2 * \log \log(n))$.

Substitution / Iteration Method

The **Iteration Method** is also known as the **Iterative Method**, **Backwards Substitution**, **Substitution Method**, and **Iterative Substitution**. It is a technique or procedure in computational mathematics used to solve a recurrence relation that uses an initial guess to generate a sequence of improving approximate solutions for a class of problems, in which the nth approximation is derived from the previous ones. In the **iteration method** we continue to "unfold" the recurrence until we "see the pattern".

Let's look at a recurrence relation problem and try to solve it. By solve it, here I mean get it in a **"closed form"**. A **Closed-Form** Solution is an equation that solves a given problem in terms of functions and mathematical operations from a given generally-accepted set. For example, an infinite sum would generally not be considered **closed-form**.

Let's start with the recurrence relation, $T(n) = 2 * T(n/2) + 2$ and try to get it in a closed form. Note that **'T'** stands for time, and therefore **T(n)** is a function of time that takes in input of size **'n'**.

$$T(n) = 2T(n/2) + 2$$

This is our first iteration, we will name our iterations as **'k'** such that the first iteration means **k=1**, and the second means **k=2** and so on. The **'k'** value will be used later.

Now we need to figure out what **T(n/2)** is. We can do that by taking "n/2" and putting it into our original function **T(n)**, to get the following:
Note: We are just replacing **n** with **n/2**.

T(n/2) = 2T((n/2) / 2) + 2
= **2T (n/4) + 2**

So, our original equation looks like the following when k= 2
T(n) = 2T(n/2) + 2
= 2(2T **(n/4) + 2**) + 2
= 4T(n/4) + 4 + 2

That was our second iteration, so this means **k=2**. Now we must figure out what **T(n/4)** is. We can do that by taking "n/4", and putting it into our original function **T(n)**, to get the following:

T(n/4) = 2T((n/4) / 2) + 2
= **2T(n/8) + 2**

So, our original equation looks like the following when k=3

$T(n) = 4T(n/4) + 4 + 2$

$= 4(\mathbf{2T(n/8) + 2}) + 4 + 2$

$= 8T(n/8) + 8 + 4 + 2$

That was our third iteration, so this means **k=3**. Now we must figure out what **T(n/8)** is. We can do that by taking "n/8", and putting it into our original function **T(n)**, to get the following:

$T(n/8) = 2T((n/8) / 2) + 2$

$= \mathbf{2T(n/16) + 2}$

So, our original equation looks like the following when k=4

$T(n) = 8T(n/8) + 8 + 4 + 2$

$= 8(\mathbf{2T(n/16) + 2}) + 8 + 4 + 2$

$= 16T(n/16) + 16 + 8 + 4 + 2$

That was our fourth iteration, so this means **k=4**. Now we must figure out what **T(n/16)** is. We can do that by taking "n/8", and putting it into our original function **T(n)**, to get the following:

$T(n/16) = 2T((n/16) / 2) + 2$

$= \mathbf{2T(n/32) + 2}$

So, our original equation looks like the following when k=5

$T(n) = 16T(n/16) + 16 + 8 + 4 + 2$

$=16(\mathbf{2T(n/32) + 2}) +16 + 8+ 4 + 2$
$= 32T(n/32) + 32 +16 + 8+ 4 + 2$

Okay let's stop here and see if we can see a pattern, if not then you should continue this method or process until you do.

When k=1, we had T(n) = 2T(n/2) + 2
When k=2, we had T(n) = 4T(n/4) + 4 + 2
When k=3, we had T(n) = 8T(n/8) + 8+ 4 + 2
When k=4, we had T(n) = 16T(n/16)+16 + 8+ 4 + 2
When k=5, we had T(n) = 32T(n/32)+ 32 +16 + 8+ 4 + 2

Let's rewrite this a little bit more to see if we can see a pattern.

When k=1, we had T(n) = 2T(n/2) + 2
$= T(n) = 2T(n/2) + 2 \rightarrow T(n) = 2T(n/2) + 2(1)$

When k=2, we had T(n) = 4T(n/4) + 4 + 2
$= T(n) = 4T(n/4) + 4 + 2 \rightarrow T(n) = 4T(n/4) + 2(2 + 1)$

When k=3, we had T(n) = 8T(n/8) + 8+ 4 + 2
$= T(n) = 8T(n/8) + 8+ 4 + 2 \rightarrow T(n) = 8T(n/8) + 2(4 + 2 +1)$

When k=4, we had T(n) = 16T(n/16) +16 + 8+ 4 + 2
= T(n) = 16T(n/16) +16 + 8+ 4 + 2 → T(n) = 16T(n/16) +2(8+ 4 + 2 +1)

When k=5, we had T(n) = 32T(n/32) + 32 +16 + 8+ 4 + 2
=T(n) = 32T(n/32) + 32 +16 + 8+ 4 + 2
= T(n) = 32T(n/32) + 2 (16 + 8+ 4 + 2 + 1)

Notice the general form in terms of 'k' looks like:

$T(n) = 2^k * T(n/(2^k)) + 2 * \sum_{i=0}^{k-1} 2^{\wedge}i$

NOTE: The below summation from the Geometric Series Formula.

$$\sum_{i=0}^{k-1} 2^i = \frac{1 - 2^i}{1 - 2} = 2^i - 1$$

So, our general form looks like below:
$T(n) = 2^k * T(n/(2^k)) + 2 *(2^k - 1)$
$T(n) = 2^k * T(n/(2^k)) + 2^{(k+1)} - 2$

When does our recurrence relation stop? Well it stops when $T(n/(2^k))$ hits the base case. You may say, but we were never given a base case. That's okay because every recurrence relation has a base case, and it is always some constant value. So, if a base case isn't provided, we can make one up. So, our base case will be **T (1) = C**, which means when our input is of size 1, the time it takes to execute the function 'T' is 'C' unit(s) of time, where 'C' is some constant unit of time. This means when n = 1, T(n=1) = C.

We must now get our T(n) function from our general form to stop, and therefore need T(n/(2^k)) =C, this implies n/(2^k) must equal 1, since T(n/(2^k) =1) = C. **Let's do some algebra below.**

= n/(2^k) = 1
= n = (2^k)
= $\log_2 n$ = k

We now not only have our stopping case but can also put our value 'k' in terms of n, for the entire equation, by plugging in 'log base 2 of n' for 'k'.

T(n) = 2^ (log base 2 of n) * T (n/ (2^ (log base 2 of n))) + 2 *($2^{\wedge}$(log base 2 of n)−1)

T(n) = n * T(n/n) + 2(n−1)
T(n) = n T (1) + 2n−2
T(n) = n*(C) + 2n−2
T(n) = Cn + 2n−2
T(n) = n (C+2)−2

So, our guess is that the closed form of our recurrence relation is:
T(n) = n (C+2)−2, where C is some constant

NOTE: n (C+2)−2 is O(n)

If C = 0 then the equation is
T(n) = n (0 + 2)−2
T(n) = 2n−2 = 2(n-1)

Because the closed form is a guess we need to show that our guess is correct and to do that we can use **Mathematical Induction**.

Induction

Mathematical induction is a special way to prove things, it is a mathematical proof technique. It is typically used to prove that a property holds true for all-natural numbers (0,1,2,3,4, …).

When doing a proof by induction, you will need 2 main components, your **base case**, and your **induction step**, and 1 optional step called the **induction hypothesis**. The **base case** shows that the statement is true for the first natural number, and the **induction step** shows that the statement is true for the next one. As for the **induction hypothesis**, it's your assumption that the statement is true for some arbitrary value.

Example:
Prove: $T(n) = 5n^2-6n$ is $O(n\text{\textasciicircum}2)$, $T(1) = 1$

 By Big-Oh definition we must show, there exist a value C and K that makes the below equation true.
$5n^2-6n \leq Cn^2$ for all n>K

Proof by Induction:
Step 1 (Base Case): Prove Base Case is true (n=1)
$T(1) = 1$ True

Step 2 (Induction Hypotheses):
We will use this later Assume: $5a^2-6a \leq Ca^2$, for all a> K is true, where 'a' is some arbitrary value. This means we assume there exists a value 'C' that makes this inequality true.

Step 3 (Induction Step):
We want to show $5(a+1)^2- 6(a+1) \leq C(a+1)^2$, this will show that this statement holds true for the next natural number.

Solve the right-hand side of the equation $5(a+1)^2- 6(a+1)$.

$$5(a+1)^2- 6(a+1) = 5a^2 + 10a + 5 - 6a - 6$$
$$= 5a^2 - 6a + 10a + 5 - 6$$
$$= 5a^2 - 6a + 10a - 1$$

Using the Induction Hypotheses $5a^2-6a \leq Ca^2$
if $5a^2-6a \leq Ca^2$ then $5a^2 - 6a + 10a - 1 \leq Ca^2 + 10a - 1$

Note: $Ca^2 + 10a - 1 \leq Ca^2 + C*2a + C$ for all $C \geq 5$ no matter what value 'a' is, this means we can choose any positive value for K.

$5a^2 - 6a + 10a - 1 \leq Ca^2 + C*2a + C$ for all $C \geq 5$

Note: $Ca^2 + C*2a + C = C(a+1)^2$

$5a^2 - 6a + 10a - 1 \leq C(a+1)^2$ for all $C \geq 5$

Therefore:
$5a^2 - 6a + 10a - 1 \leq Ca^2 + 10a - 1 \leq C(a+1)^2$

Step 4 (Conclusion):
$5a^2 - 6a + 10a - 1 \leq Ca^2 + 10a - 1 \leq C(a+1)^2$
$5(a+1)^2 - 6(a+1) = 5a^2 - 6a + 10a - 1$, we have proven
$5(a+1)^2 - 6(a+1) \leq C(a+1)^2$,

therefore **$5n^2-6n$ is $O(n^2)$**

Change of Variable

There are many ways to solve a recurrence relation runtime. One way to do this is a method called "change of variable". Domain transformations can sometimes be used to substitute a function for the argument of the relation and make it easier to solve. The idea is to select a function for S(m), when given T(n).

Let's look at an example:

$$T(n) = 2T(\sqrt{n}) + \log n$$

Let's rewrite the equation by substituting m=log n, and then plug it back in to the recurrence to get the following:

$$T(2^m) = 2T(2^{\frac{m}{2}}) + m$$

Now we will create a new function called 'S' that takes in a parameter 'm' such that S(m) = T(2^m).

$$S(m) = T(2^m)$$

This means that S(m) = 2T($2^{(m/2)}$) + m.

$$S(m) = 2T(2^{\frac{m}{2}}) + m$$

If S(m) = T(2^m) then S(m-1) = T($2^{(m-1)}$) and S(m/2) = T($2^{(m/2)}$), so we can rewrite our function to get the following:

$$S(m) = 2S(m/2) + m$$

Now we can use another technique like the Master Theorem to solve for **'S'**. Once we use this technique we easily see that **'S'** belongs to **O(m log m)**.

This means that our original function **'T'** belongs to **O(log n * log (log n))**, since we can simply replace **'m'** with **'log n'** because **m=log n**

Change Recursion Function to Recurrence Relation

We can solve a recursive function, by changing it into a recurrence relation. Let's look at a recursive program called "pow" that takes in two integers 'x' and 'n', and then returns x^n, so this means that pow(2,3) = 2^3=8.

Recursion Function:

```
int pow(int x, int n){
//Base Case
if (n== 0)
    return 1;
else// Recursive Case
    return pow(x, n-1) * x;
}
```

Change the recursion program to a recurrence relation:

$T(0) = C_1$, C_1 is some constant amount of time to return a number, since the base case returns 1;

$T(n) = T(n-1) + C_2$, since the recursive case returns pow(x, n-1) we get $T(n-1)$ plus the time to execute x, because we multiply pow(x, n-1) by x which takes some constant amount of time C_2.

Change Function to Recurrence Relation

Usually when analyzing programs, we start with a recursive definition of the program and try to figure out a closed form or function for the recursive definition and then solve it's time complexity. Here we are doing the opposite, we are starting with the closed form or function and changing it to a recursive definition.

Below we have our problem or function that we want to change into a recursive definition.

$f(n) = 2^n + 1$

The base case is the terminating case in recursion, that doesn't use recursion to give an answer. The base case here is when n=0, to get f(0) = 2.

Base Case: Try to solve for n=0

$f(0) = 2^0 + 1$
$= 1 + 1$
$= 2$

The recursive case is the case when the function defines itself. Here we try to create a recursive case for our function $f(n) = 2^n + 1$. If $f(n) = 2^n + 1$ then $f(n+1) = 2^{(n+1)} + 1$.

Recursive Case: Try to solve f(n)

$f(n+1) = 2^{(n+1)} + 1$

$= 2 * 2^n + 1$

$= (2 * 2^n) + 1$

$= (2^n + 2^n) + 1$

$= 2^n + 2^n + 1$

$= 2^n + 2^n + 1 + 0$

$= 2^n + 2^n + 1 + 1 - 1$

$= 2^n + 1 + 2^n + 1 - 1$

$= (2^n + 1) + (2^n + 1) - 1$

$= f(n) + f(n) - 1$

$f(n+1) = f(n) + f(n) - 1$

$f(n+1 - 1) = f(n)$

$f(n + 1 - 1) = f(n-1) + f(n-1) - 1$

$f(n) = f(n-1) + f(n-1) - 1$

$f(n) = 2f(n-1) - 1$

Conclusion:

The recursive definition for $f(n) = 2^n + 1$ is below.

$f(0) = 2$

$f(n) = 2f(n-1) - 1$

This function time complexity is of course $O(2^n)$

Chapter 6: Algorithm analysis cheat codes

6.1 Recurrence Relation Cheats

In this chapter I plan on showing / summarizing some simple techniques and memorizations that can be used to simplify solving an algorithms time complexity. Have you found it hard to solve the time complexity of recurrence relations? I will show you how to solve some of the most common recurrence relations fast and easily without using any techniques other than memorization.

Below are the common recurrences.

Note: a, b, d and k are all constant values.

1. $T(n) = T(n-1)+b$, $T(1) = a$
   $T(n) = \Theta(n)$

2. $T(n) = T(n-1) + bn$, $T(1) = a$
   $T(n) = \Theta(n^2)$

3. $T(n) = T(n/2) + b$, $T(1) = a$
   $T(n) = \Theta(\log n)$

4. $T(n) = T(n/2) + bn$, $T(1) = a$
   $T(n) = \Theta(n)$

5. $T(n) = kT(n/k) + b$, $T(1) = a$
   $T(n) = \Theta(n)$

6. $T(n) = kT(n/k) + bn$, $T(1) = a$
   $T(n) = \Theta(n \log n)$

7. $T(n) = T(n-1) + T(n-2) + d$, $T(1) = a$, $T(2) = b$
   $T(n) = \Theta(2^n)$

8. $T(n) = T(n-1) + bn^k$, $T(1) = a$
   $T(n) = \Theta(n^{k+1})$

Fun Fact:
The recurrence relation below equates to the following summation.

$T(n) = T(n-1) + bn^k$, $T(1) = a$
$T(n) = \Theta(n^{k+1})$

$$\sum_{i=0}^{n} i^k$$

You can learn more about this by looking up Faulhaber's formula or sums of power!

6.2 Limits to Solve Asymptotic

Although this technique is a little advanced, it is an easy way to solve Big – O, Little -O, Big Theta, Big Omega or Little Omega. In calculus, a **limit** is the value that a function or sequence "approaches" as the input or index approaches some value.

Lim f(n) / g(n) = L
n→∞

If L= 0 or a constant value 'C' then f(n) is O(g(n))
If L= infinity or a constant value 'C' then f(n) is Ω(g(n))
If L= a constant value 'C' then f(n) is Θ(g(n))
If L= 0 then f(n) is o(g(n))
If L = infinity then f(n) is ω(g(n))

Example:
Prove that 2n + 1 is Θ(n)
f(n) = 2n + 1
g(n) = n

Lim f(n) / g(n) = L
n→∞

$= \text{Lim}_{\;n\to\infty} \; 2n+1 \; / \; n = L$

$= \text{Lim}_{\;n\to\infty} \; 2n \; / \; n + \text{Lim}_{\;n\to\infty} \; 1 \; / \; n = L$

$= \text{Lim}_{\;n\to\infty} \; 2 + 0 = L$

$= 2 + 0 = L$

$= 2 = L$

By case 3 If L= a constant value 'C' then f(n) is $\Theta(g(n))$, L=2 which is a constant, therefore 2n + 1 is **$\Theta(n)$**, which implies that it is also **O(n)** and **$\Omega(n)$**.

6.3 Loops

The below are a few loops and there running time, where a,c,e< n, and b,d,f > 0.

O(n)
for(int i=a; i<n; i+=b){//Some Constant Work}

O(n²)
for(int i=a; i<n; i+=b)
  for(int j=c; j<n; j+=d)
    {//Some Constant Work}

O(n²)
for(int i=a; i<n*n; i+=b)
  {//Some Constant Work}

O(n³)
for(int i=a; i<n; i+=b)
  for(int j=c; j<n; j+=d)
    for(int k=e; k<n; k+=f)
    {//Some Constant Work}

O(n³)
for(int i=a; i<n*n*n; i+=b)
  {//Some Constant Work}

6.4 Sets

Big Theta
1) $An + B = \Theta(n)$, where $A >= 1$, and $B >= 0$
2) $An^2 + Bn + C = \Theta(n^2)$, where $A >= 1$, and $B, C >= 0$
3) $An^k + Bn^{k-1} + ... + C = \Theta(n^k)$, where $A >= 1$, and $B, C >= 0$

Big - O
1) $An + B = O(n)$, where $A >= 1$, and $B >= 0$
2) $An^2 + Bn + C = O(n^2)$, where $A >= 1$, and $B, C >= 0$
3) $An^k + Bn^{k-1} + ... + C = O(n^k)$, where $A >= 1$, and $B, C >= 0$

Chapter 7:
Practice problems

7.1 Algorithm Analysis Problems

1) What is the running time of the following recurrence relation code snippet?

T(1)= 1

T(n)= T(n-1) + n

(A) O(n)

(B) $\Omega(n^2)$

(C) $\Theta(1)$

(D) All of the above

We can use the substitution / iteration method to solve this recurrence relation.

(K) Iteration

----

(1) T(n) = T(n-1) + n

Now we need to solve for T(n-1) by substituting (n-1) for n in the original equation:

   T(n-1) = T(n-2) +(n-1)

We will substitute it back into the original equation. This substitution gives us the equation for the second K iteration K=2

(2) $T(n) = T(n-2) + (n-1) + n$
$= T(n-2) + n - 1 + n$
$= T(n-2) + 2n - 1$

Now we need to solve for $T(n-2)$ by substituting $(n-2)$ for n in the original equation:

$T(n-2) = T(n-3) + (n-2)$

We will substitute it back into the original equation. This substitution gives us the equation for the third K iteration K=3

(3) $T(n) = T(n-3) + (n-2) + 2n - 1$
$= T(n-3) + n - 2 + 2n - 1$
$= T(n-3) + 3n - 3$

Now we need to solve for $T(n-3)$ by substituting $(n-3)$ for n in the original equation:

$T(n-3) = T(n-4) + (n-3)$

We will substitute it back into the original equation. This substitution gives us the equation for the fourth K iteration K=4

(4) $T(n) = T(n-4) + (n-3) + 3n - 3$
$= T(n-4) + n - 3 + 3n - 3$
$= T(n-4) + 4n - 6$

We have 4 equations, and we want to solve for a closed (Not defined in terms of itself) form, but first we will need to find the general form. Using the k iterations, look for a pattern. If you don't see a pattern go to the next k iteration until you do:

At K=1, $T(n) = T(n-1) + 1n - (0)$
At K=2, $T(n) = T(n-2) + 2n - (1 + 0)$
At K=3, $T(n) = T(n-3) + 3n - (2 + 1 + 0)$
At K=4, $T(n) = T(n-4) + 4n - (3 + 2 + 1 + 0)$

General Form:
$T(n) = T(n-K) + Kn - \sum_{i=0}^{k-1} i$

Note: You can plug in k=1,2,3, or 4 in the general form and you will get the above equations.

To get rid of the recursion "T(n-k)", solve for n, in the base case:
$T(n-k=1)=1$, we want n-k=1, because $T(1) = 1$
$T(n-1=k)$, so we can replace k with n-1

Rewriting the equation above we get the closed form:

$T(n) = T(n-(n-1)) + (n-1)n - \sum_{i=0}^{(n-1)-1} i$

$\quad = T(1) + (n^2 - n) - \sum_{i=0}^{n-2} i$

$\quad = 1 + (n^2 - n) - (n-2)(n-2+1)/2$

$\quad = 1 + (n^2 - n) - (n-2)(n-1)/2$

$\quad = 2/2 + 2(n^2 - n)/2 - (n-2)(n-1)/2$

$\quad = (2 + 2(n^2 - n) - (n-2)(n-1))/2$

$\quad = (2 + 2n^2 - 2n - (n^2 - n - 2n + 2))/2$

$\quad = (2 + 2n^2 - 2n - n^2 + n + 2n - 2))/2$

$\quad = (2n^2 - n^2 - 2n + 2n + n + 2 - 2))/2$

$\quad = (n^2 + n)/2$

So, our guess is that the recurrence relation running time is $\Theta(n^2)$ since $(n^2 + n)/2$ is **$\Theta(n^2)$.** We would have to use something like proof by induction to prove that our guess is correct. It is correct.

Answer: B, the recurrence $T(n)$ equates to $n(n+1)/2 =$ $(n^2 + n)/2$ by using the iteration/substitution method which is $\Theta(n^2)$. $\Theta(n^2)$ implies that the function is also $O(n^2)$ and $\Omega(n^2)$, by the definition of what it means for a function to be $\Theta(n^2)$.

2) What is the running time of the following recurrence relation?

T(1)= 1

T(n)= T(n-1) + n²

(A) $\Theta(n^3)$

(B) $O(n^4)$

(C) $\Omega(n^2)$

(D)All of the above

Here we could use the iteration method again to solve this and find that it equals **[n(n+1)(2n+1)]/6** or we can use the "cheat" provided below:

If $T(n) = T(n-1) + bn^k$, $T(1) = a$
Then $T(n) = \Theta(n^{k+1})$

So our equation is:
T(n)= T(n-1) + n² , T(1) = 1
= T(n-1) + 1n² , T(1) = 1

This means a=1, b=1, and k=2, therefore, $T(n) = \Theta(n^{2+1}) = \Theta(n^3)$.

Answer: D, the recurrence T(n) equates to $[n(n+1)(2n+1)]/6 = (n^3)/3 + (n^2)/2 + n/6$ by using the iteration/substitution method the recurrence is $\Theta(n^3)$. This means the recurrence is also $O(n^3)$ which means it is also $O(n^4)$ or anything bigger than $O(n^3)$ and this also means the recurrence is $\Omega(n^3)$ which means the recurrence is also $\Omega(n^2)$ and anything smaller like $\Omega(n^1)$

3) What is the running time of the following recurrence relation?

$T(1)= 1$

$T(n)= T(n-1) + n^4$

(A)$\Theta(n^5)$

(B) $O(n^5)$

(C) $\Omega(n^5)$

(D) All of the above

Answer: D, the recurrence $T(n)$ belongs to $\Theta(n^5)$, which implies it belongs to Big O and Big Omega of n^5.

4) What is the running time of the following summation?

$$\sum_{i=0}^{n} i$$

(A) $O(n^2)$

(B) $\Omega(n^3)$

(C) $\Theta(n)$

(D) All of the above

We can solve this by solving the summation.

$$\sum_{i=0}^{n} i = \frac{n(n+1)}{2} = \frac{(n^2+n)}{2}$$

Answer: A, $(n^2 +n)/2$ is $\Theta(n^2)$ which means it's both $\Omega(n^2)$ and **O(n^2).**

5) What is the running time of the following summation?

$$\sum_{i=0}^{n} i^4$$

(A) $O(n^4)$

(B) $\Omega(n^3)$

(C) $\Theta(n)$

(D) All of the above

Here we can use the cheat sheet and realize the following: $T(n) = \Theta(n^{k+1})$, for the following summation.

$$\sum_{i=0}^{n} i^k$$

Our k-value equals 4, therefore the summation belongs to $\Theta(n^{k+1}) = \Theta(n^{4+1}) = \Theta(n^5)$

Answer: B, now that we know the summation is $\Theta(n^5)$, this means it's also $\mathbf{\Omega(n^3)}$, because $n^5 \geq C^* n^3$ whenever n>k is always true no matter what the positive value n is.

6) What is the running time of the following function?

$$f(x) = x^{89}$$

(A) $O(x)$

(B) $\Omega(x)$

(C) $\Theta(x)$

(D) All of the above

Answer: B, the running time of this function is $\Theta(x^{89})$, this implies that it's both $O(x^{89})$ and $\Omega(x^{89})$. Since it's $\Omega(x^{89})$ this also means it's any function that grows slower than x^{89} such as x^{88} or x^{70} or x^4 or x^1.

7) What is the running time of the following program?

```
int add( int x) {

if( x == 1)
        return 5;
    else
        return add(x -1) + 1;
}
```

(A) O(n)
(B) Θ(n)
(C) Ω (n)
(D) All of the above

Answer: D, Rewriting the code to a recurrence relation, we get T(x) = T(x-1) + 1, T(1) = 1, then we can solve by using iteration/substitution method and by doing so we get T(x) = x

8) What is the running time of the following equation?

$$\Theta(1) + \Theta(2) + \Theta(n * \log n) + \Theta(n\wedge 2) + \Theta(\log n) + \Theta(n!) = ?$$

(A) $\Theta(n^2)$
(B) $\Theta(n!)$
(C) $\Theta(3)$
(D) $\Theta(2^n)$

Answer: B, based off the order of growth $\Theta(n!)$ grows faster than all the rest therefore the fastest this equation can grow is $\Theta(n!)$.

9) What is the running time of the following equation?

$$\Theta(1) + \Theta(2) + \Theta(\log n) + \Theta(n) + \Theta(n^{56}) + \Theta(n^2) + \Theta(2^n) + \Theta(n!) = ?$$

(A) $\Theta(n)$

(B) $\Theta(n!)$

(C) $\Theta(3)$

(D) $\Theta(2^n)$

Answer: B, based off the order of growth $\Theta(n!)$ grows faster than all the rest, therefore the fastest this equation can grow is $\Theta(n!)$.

10) What is the running time of the following function?

$f(n) = n^3 + n^2 + 2$

(A) $\Theta(n)$

(B) $O(n!)$

(C) $\Theta(n!)$

(D) Both A and B

Answer: B, this function running time is $\Theta(n^3)$, which means it is also $O(n^3)$ and that means that it is Big-O of any function that grows faster than n^3 such as n^4 or n^{65} or 2^n or n!

11) What is the running time of the following function?

f(n, m)= m + n

(A) $\Theta(n + m)$
(B) $O(n^5)$
(C) $\Theta(1)$
(D) All of the above

Answer: A, This simply equates to $\Theta(n + m)$, just like f(n) = n equates to $\Theta(n)$. Except this time, we have two inputs.

12) What is the running time of the following function?

$$f(n) = \Theta(n) + n^2$$

(A) $\Theta(n)$
(B) $\Theta(n^3)$
(C) $\Theta(1)$
(D) $\Theta(n^2)$

Answer: D, we can just look at this equation and use the order of growth to figure this out. $\Theta(n)$ is some function in the form of An + B, $\Theta(n^2)$ is some function in the form $An^2 + Bn + C$ where A, B, and C are some arbitrary positive constants. So, we can rewrite this in one of two ways, 1) $f(n) = n^2 + n$ or 2) $f(n) = \Theta(n) + \Theta(n^2)$. Both equate to $\Theta(n^2)$

13) What is the running time of the following function?

$f(n) = n^3 + n + 67 + 2$

(A) $\Omega(n^3)$

(B) $O(n^3)$

(C) $\Theta(n)$

(D) Both A and B

Answer: D, because it's $\Theta(n^3)$ which implies it is both $\Omega(n^3)$ and $O(n^3)$

14) What is the running time of the following function?

$f(n)= n + n^2 + 1234$

(A) $\Theta(n^2)$

(B) $O(n)$

(C) $O(n^{67})$

(D) Both A and C

Answer: D, this is a tricky problem. We can immediately see that the function $f(n)$ is $\Theta(n^2)$ as n^2 is the highest order. What may not be so obvious is that it's also $O(n^{\text{anything greater than or equal to 2}})$, since $n^2 \leq C* n^{\text{anything greater than or equal to 2}}$ whenever $n > k$.

15) What is the running time of the following function?

$f(n) = n^3 + n^2 + 2$

(A) $\Theta(n^4)$

(B) $O(n!)$

(C) $\Theta(n^5)$.

(D) $\Omega(n!)$

Answer: B, this is a little tricky. We know the function itself is $\Theta(n^3)$, but that isn't an option. It cannot be $\Theta(n^4)$ or $\Theta(n!)$ because it's $\Theta(n^3)$. By the definition of Big-O, we realize $\Theta(n^3) \leq \Theta(n!) \rightarrow n^3 \leq C*n!$ for all $n > k$. This means our function is **O(n!)**.

16) What is the running time of the following recurrence?

$T(n) = T(2n/3) + 1$, $T(0) = 6787$

(A) $\Theta(\log n)$

(B) $\Theta(n \log n)$

(C) $\Theta(n^2)$

(D) $\Theta(2n/3)$

Here we can use the Master Theorem / Master Method to solve this recurrence relation.

Given A Recurrence Equation in the form:
$T(n) = AT(n/B) + \Theta(n^C * \log n)$

Case 1 to solve the function running time:
If $C < \log_B A$ then $T(n) = \Theta(n^{\log_B A})$

Case 2 to solve the function running time:
If $C = \log_B A$ then $T(n) = \Theta(n^C * \log^{k+1}(n))$, for $k > -1$

Case 3 to solve the function running time:
If $C > \log_B A$ then $T(n) = \Theta(n^C)$

The equation we want to solve is:
$T(n) = T(2n/3) + 1$

Let's get it in the same form as the master Theorem:
$T(n) = 1 \cdot T(n/(3/2)) + n^0 \cdot \log^0 n$

This means $A=1$, $b=(3/2)$, $k=0$ and $c=0$

NOTE: $\log^0 n = 1$
NOTE: $b = (3/2)$, because $n/(3/2) = 2n/3$

Next, we check the three cases, and since all three cases involve $\log_B A$ to be compared with C, we will go ahead and solve for that first. $\log_{(3/2)} 1 = 0$.

NOTE: $\log_{(3/2)} 1 = 0$, because $(3/2)^0 = 1$

So, $C=0$ and this is equal to $\log_{(3/2)} 1 = 0$, and $k > -1$, this means Case 2 is true.

Case 2 states: If $C = \log_B A$ then $T(n) = \Theta(n^C \cdot \log^{k+1}(n)) \rightarrow$ If $0=0$ Then $T(n) = \Theta(n^0 \cdot \log^{0+1}(n)) = \Theta(1 \cdot \log^1 n) = \Theta(\log n)$

Answer: A, Using the Master Theorem, we see the recurrence relation is $\Theta(\log n)$. Notice we do not actually need to know the base case value since it is always a constant.

17) What is the running time of the following recurrence?

$$T(n) = 4T(n/2) + n$$

(A) $\Theta(\log n)$

(B) $\Theta(n \log n)$

(C) $\Theta(n^2)$

(D) $\Theta(2n/3)$

Answer: C, Use the Master Theorem Case 1, and we see the answer is $\Theta(n^{\log_2 4}) = \Theta(n^2)$.

Concluding Thoughts

You should now be armed with an approach to solve and analyze many algorithms. I hope the writing and math problems here were helpful. Keep up the learning!

www.ingramcontent.com/pod-product-compliance
Lightning Source LLC
LaVergne TN
LVHW092336060326
832902LV00008B/679